Why Does Water Freeze?

Peter Rees

and other questions about matter

WHY IS IT SO?
?
Science

CAMBRIDGE
UNIVERSITY PRESS

Contents

Questions about matter

The bubbles in soft drinks are gas.

Q: What is everything made of?

A: Everything you can see or touch is made of matter. Your body is made of matter. Your food is made of matter. Even the air you breathe is matter! Matter can be any size, shape or colour.

Q: What kinds of matter are there?

A: There are different kinds of matter. Solids are **dense** and you cannot usually pour them. Stones and crayons are solids. You can pour liquids and gases. Orange juice and honey are liquids. We can feel liquids, but often we cannot feel gases because the **particles** are so spread out.

Q: How do you know something is a solid?

A: Solids are hard and do not change shape. Solids can be different colours like crayons and glass beads. They can also feel very different from each other. Some solids feel rough like rocks, but other solids are smooth like glass.

There are some solids that can pour, for example, sugar, sand, coffee and salt. These are made up of very small particles.

Questions about substances

Q: Why is water wet?

A: Water feels wet because it is a liquid. Liquids are made up of tiny pieces of matter that are only loosely joined up. They can flow over and around us. They stick to our skin and make us feel wet. We can rub the water off with a towel to get dry again.

Q: Why does water freeze?

A: Water freezes when it is very, very cold. Tiny pieces of matter stick together to make ice. When ice gets warm, the heat makes the pieces move again so it **melts** and turns back into water.

Q: What is air made of?

Air is mainly made up of the gases **oxygen** and **nitrogen**. These gases in air are needed for life on Earth. People and other animals breathe in oxygen. Plants produce oxygen.

Q: What makes fire burn?

Oxygen makes fire burn. When **fuel** is heated up in oxygen, it gets so hot that it starts to break apart. The parts join with the oxygen to make new matter. Burning produces heat and light.

Fire facts

Different fuels make different coloured flames. Most candles have yellow flames, but a gas cooker has a blue flame.

It's a fact

> Tiny atoms

Atoms are so tiny that millions of them would fit on a full stop! Two or more atoms joined together are called molecules. Matter is made up of atoms and molecules.

Gold is a mineral that is in the ground.

> Minerals

Minerals are natural substances in the ground, such as gold, tin and salt. Rocks are made of minerals.

Sea water contains the mineral salt.

> Quicksilver

Mercury is a liquid metal which is sometimes called quicksilver. It is used inside **barometers**.

> Making glass

Glass is made from sand. The sand is heated until it melts and changes into a liquid. When it cools down, it turns into glass.

> Making fog

Dry ice is a gas that is frozen solid. As it **thaws**, it changes back into a gas. The cold gas looks like fog so it is often used in scary films or in stage shows.

Can you believe it?

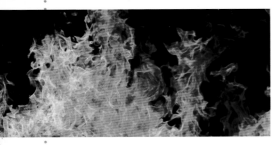

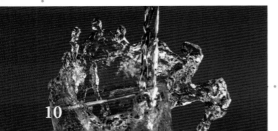

Tar

Tar is a black liquid that feels like a solid. You can pick it up and you can even break it. Tar is so thick that it takes a long time to pour even a small amount. It is used for making roads.

The four elements

The ancient Greeks believed everything was made up of air, earth, fire and water. They called these the four **elements**. They thought the elements were mixed in different ways to make different kinds of matter. Today scientists know of more than 110 different elements.

Rock can melt!

All solids can melt if you heat them up enough – even rock! Lava in a volcano is just molten rock at about 1,000° centigrade.

Diamonds in your pencil?

The lead in pencils is not really lead. It is mainly graphite. Graphite is a soft, black mineral. When it is heated and squeezed very, very hard, it changes into diamond!

Magic slime

You can make a special slime by mixing together 4 eggcups of water, 8 eggcups of cornflour and some food colouring. The slime feels like a liquid when you put your hand in it, but feels solid when you drop it, push it or make it into a ball.

11

Who found out?

Atoms: Democritus

The ancient Greek philosopher, Democritus (about 460–370 BCE) was the first person to say that everything is made from atoms. He believed that all matter was made of elements, which he called *atomos*. This is where our word 'atom' comes from.

More about atoms: John Dalton

An English chemist and physicist called John Dalton (1766–1844) found out that there are many different kinds of atoms. He drew pictures of how he thought each atom looked. He decided that all matter must consist of small particles.

Plastic: John Wesley Huff

John Wesley Huff (1837–1920) was an American who invented one of the first plastics. Plastics are **artificial** materials and are used to make many everyday objects, for example, toys and containers. Plastics are cheap, strong and last for a long time.

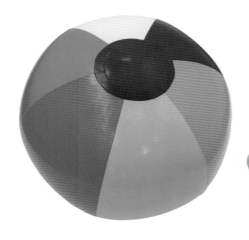

It's quiz time!

1 **Join the beginnings and endings of the words to make whole words.**

lids   oxy   li   quid

as   gen   go   mat   ter

so

2 **Now use the words to complete the sentences.**

1. Everything is made of __ __ __ __ __ __.

2. Animals breathe in __ __ __ __ __ __.

3. Water is a __ __ __ __ __ __.

4. The bubbles in soft drinks are a __ __ __ .

5. Rocks, tables and spoons are __ __ __ __ __ __ .

3 **Six words from the book are hidden in this wordsearch. Can you find them?**

Which is the odd one out? Why?

L	U	N	C	H	B	O	X
L	V	H	M	O	Y	T	U
A	R	I	J	N	D	F	S
Q	O	K	R	E	E	P	U
O	C	R	A	Y	O	N	G
B	K	L	T	S	J	R	A
S	A	N	D	G	W	E	R

_____

_____

_____

_____

4 Draw lines to match the questions and answers.

1. Who was the first person to say that everything is made from atoms?

2. What is gold?

3. What happens to water when it gets very cold?

4. What is tar?

5. What happens when ice gets warm?

a) A mineral.

b) It freezes.

c) Democritus.

d) It melts.

e) A liquid.

5 True (T) or false (F)? Correct the false ones.

1. Matter can be any size, shape or colour. __T__

_____

2. Often we cannot feel gases because they are spread out. ____

_____

3. Water freezes when it is very, very hot. ____

_____

4. Freezing produces heat and light. ____

_____

5. Only six atoms can fit on a full stop. ____

_____

Glossary

artificial: made by people

barometer: an instrument that measures air pressure and shows when the weather is going to change

dense: thickly or closely packed together

elements: substances that are made up of only one kind of atom

fuel: something that burns

melt: change from solid to liquid by being heated

nitrogen: a colourless gas forming about 78 per cent of Earth's atmosphere

oxygen: a gas that humans and animals breathe

particles: tiny pieces of matter

thaw: change from a frozen solid by being heated